AF571759

Bellevue Farm

Bellevue Farm

EXPLORING VIRGINIA'S
COASTAL COUNTRYSIDE

Curtis J. Badger

STACKPOLE
BOOKS

Published by
STACKPOLE BOOKS
5067 Ritter Road
Mechanicsburg, PA 17055

Printed in the United States of America

10 9 8 7 6 5 4 3 2 1

First edition

Artwork by Peter H. Ring

Library of Congress Cataloging-in-Publication Data

Badger, Curtis J.
Bellevue Farm: exploring Virginia's coastal countryside / Curtis J. Badger.
p. cm.
Includes bibliographical references (p.).
ISBN 0-8117-0226-X (hc)
1. Natural history—Virginia—Bellevue Farm. 2. Bellevue Farm (Va.) I. Title.
QH105.V8B3 1997
508.755'1—dc20 96-23308
CIP

To Tom and Lynn,
who have shared many happy hours
with me on Bellevue Farm

Contents

Acknowledgments

I would like to thank most of all my wife, Lynn, and son, Tom, who have shared with me many adventures at Bellevue Farm. They also share my curiosity, sense of wonder, and eagerness to learn more about the flora and fauna of this special place.

To The Nature Conservancy, owner of Bellevue Farm, I would like to express my gratitude for four years of unlimited access. Special thanks are due John Hall, director of the Conservancy's Virginia Coast Reserve, who not only gave me permission to explore the farm, but also read this manuscript and made numerous valuable suggestions. Thanks also to Terry Thompson, director of research and education at the Virginia Coast Reserve, who made sure this amateur got his facts straight.

The Eastern Shore Public Library provided me with numerous documents relating to the Parramore family, the history of Bellevue Farm, and the American Indian presence on the Eastern Shore.

Thanks, too, to Judith Schnell of Stackpole Books, my friend and editor, for her support, editorial skills, and wise counsel.

Bellevue Farm

Four years ago I began to spend a great deal of time on a large seaside farm on the coast of Virginia. The farm is called Bellevue, and it is owned by The Nature Conservancy. It is part of the Conservancy's Virginia Coast Reserve, a sanctuary of fourteen barrier islands, vast salt marshes, and adjacent upland farms. The sanctuary comprises more than forty-five thousand acres and covers fifty miles of coastline. It is, as I wrote in *Salt Tide: Cycles and Currents of Life Along the Coast,* the last of the coastal wilderness on the eastern seaboard of the United States. But it is more than a remnant—it is a fully functioning barrier island lagoon system, a place that remains today much as it was when Europeans established their first permanent settlement here in 1620.

Bellevue is only a small part of the Virginia Coast Reserve, and it is something of a stepchild, having come under Conservancy ownership in 1984 as part of a transaction with another conservation organization that offered the Conservancy its holdings with the stipulation that it take all or none.

The Conservancy took all, because the package included some important sites near the headquarters of the Virginia Coast Reserve, Brownsville Farm on Hog Island Bay, some thirty miles south of Bellevue.

I began spending time at Bellevue through an informal arrangement with the director of the Virginia Coast Reserve, John Hall. John needed someone to keep an eye on the farm, and I needed a place to explore. It was a marriage of convenience.

I was drawn to Bellevue Farm because of its remarkable natural diversity. It is a large farm, more than twelve hundred acres, but much of it is salt marsh. It is in the shape of a peninsula, with Burton's Bay on one side and Finney Creek on another. A dirt lane leaves the county road, crosses the cultivated fields, passes an old house lot and cemetery, and meanders through a pine woods before it comes to an end at a place called Channel Point, the very tip of the peninsula, where Finney Creek deepens and widens and empties into Burton's Bay.

Along the way, one passes thick hedgerows with quail and raccoons and yellow-rumped warblers. There is a grove of persimmon trees where the opossums come for dinner. Deer trails run parallel to the hedgerows, and in winter Canada geese and snow geese come at dawn to green fields of wheat.

There is an old pine woods—not virgin growth, but old nonetheless—and among the big trees, on the marshy shore, I find the charred stumps of the previous generation of pines, still thick and heavy with resins after sixty years. Each fall I pull a few stumps out and cut them into strips of fatwood, an excellent starter for the woodstove.

On the east side of the farm are the wide, shallow waters

of Burton's Bay. Brant gather there in winter to feed on submerged grasses. Mergansers dive for killifish. Yellowlegs whistle at me when I walk the shoreline.

Across the bay is Cedar Island, one of the last privately held barrier beaches, and farther south, across a narrow inlet, is Parramore Island, part of the Virginia Coast Reserve. Parramore and Bellevue have an interesting link in that Bellevue was the home of Colonel William Parramore, who helped frame America's move toward independence, and his son Thomas, who fought in the American Revolution. The Parramores owned the island, which no doubt was part of the *belle vue*—beautiful view—they enjoyed from their second-floor windows.

Colonel William, his wife, Sarah, their son Thomas and his wife, Mary Darby, and other family members are buried in the cemetery at the farm, which until recently had been overgrown beyond recognition. My wife, Lynn, and I, with several friends, spent a day last spring removing fallen trees, honeysuckle, and greenbrier, discovering in the process additional graves and an ancient brick wall that surrounds the burial ground. We have since cleaned the marble grave markers and reassembled concrete slabs that had been broken. Our efforts last year were rewarded this spring, as hundreds of jonquils bloomed for probably the first time in decades.

The southern boundary of the farm is Finney Creek, a meandering tidal creek with dozens of little branches that emerge rhizomelike from the main stem, reaching far into the land, creating little marshy ditches called guts and drains.

All of these habitats are worth exploring, for varying reasons. When I first began going to the farm, I did so to have a place to walk or to hunt. But I found that in walking or hunting I was missing too much; I was seeing the big picture but

Peter Ring © 1996

missing all the vital small details. So I learned to slow down, to take my exercise by jogging around the block in the neighborhood where we live but to approach Bellevue in shuffling steps, covering little ground, or sometimes none at all. Instead of a gun I brought binoculars.

In the four years I have been exploring Bellevue Farm, I find that my pace has slowed, my focus has narrowed, but my fascination with the land has expanded. My relationship with Bellevue began with long afternoon hikes, muscle-stretching walks that ended the workday. And then I began to search the hedgerows for songbirds, to stalk the honeysuckle thickets looking for saplings for walking sticks, to collect fatwood. Exploring the cemetery and the old house site brought me into the lives of the Parramores, the ghosts of the farm who lived on this land when America was part of the British empire. Finding stone tools in plowed fields brought in an even earlier human presence. And recently I've found that exploring the farm is no longer a matter of exercise, or a study of natural history or of human history. It deals with discovering something elemental in oneself, a retreat into some dimly lit aspect of consciousness where the realm of nature enables one to look inward with increasing clarity.

I have learned over the past four years to look for detail, to narrow my view but also to broaden my perception, to become more open. I am not a scientist and do not have the ability and patience to concentrate on a specific natural community or species. Rather, I set out, in a very naive way, to learn all I could about a single old farm, and this forced me to look at an increasingly broader picture, one that included the past as well as the present, and one that called upon the imagination to supply certain details that time had erased.

This book, then, is an amateur naturalist's account of

exploring a farm, of learning about nature. In this sense it looks outward, discovering and defining things. But in the four years I have worked on this book, I have found that it also has been a journey inward. My time spent at Bellevue has taught me much about nature and even a few things about myself.

Follow the Water

I find that the older I get, the more I enjoy hunting with binoculars or camera instead of a shotgun.

Yesterday I decided to take Smoke down to Bellevue Farm to look for quail, but in the peculiar and unpredictable ways of bird dogs, he declined to go. What happened was this. I was sitting in the truck with the door open, getting ready to start the engine and let it warm up before loading Smoke. The dog jumped up on me just as I turned the switch key and the truck rumbled to life. Smoke apparently thought that he either had committed some grievous wrong or was in grave danger and quickly retreated to his doghouse, refusing to come out.

Just as well, I thought. I put the shotgun away, picked up the binoculars and microcassette recorder, stuck an orange in the pocket of my hunting vest, and was on my way.

I have tried taking notes and making field sketches when I'm on my hikes, but I find the process intrusive. It interferes with my enjoyment of the things I see and hear. I'm too clumsy to hold a notepad and look through the binoculars at the same time, and besides, I can't draw.

So I've become attached to my little recorder, which fits in my shirt pocket and will even pick up bird songs. I talk to myself when I discover things in the woods, and when I play the recording later I can relive the experience.

My recorded notes from yesterday began with a flock of cedar waxwings, which were flitting between the cedars that line the farm road and a huge holly tree bejeweled with red berries. Beautiful birds, I noted, even though the day was heavily overcast and the subtle colors were not visible. The gray crest and stylish black mask give the bird the look of a pirate hero from a forties operetta. They moved in unison in a flock of about twenty-five, fluttering down to drink in a puddle, then returning as one to the cedars or holly.

Two hawks in the distance were circling and diving at each other. One was larger than the other, fan-tailed, a buteo, perhaps a red-tailed hawk. The other . . . I don't know, maybe a Cooper's.

The two birds disappeared beyond the woods, but in about five minutes the redtail was back, and I could see it up close, a big, beautiful, mature female bird whose rust-colored tail shone brilliantly despite the clouds. She drove off the smaller accipiter and now was going to hunt the woods herself.

A pine woods separates two farm fields, and a stream runs the length of the woods, which is about one hundred yards wide. The hawk began at the west end of the woods, gliding into the wind, pumping her wings just enough to maintain airspeed. I told my recorder that her primary feathers were spread like fingers, moving slightly to help balance her in flight.

The hawk screamed as she hunted the line of woods, a

Peter Ring ©1996

piercing cry that sounded like a small mammal in great agony. On a quiet day, the hawk's screech would carry for miles. My recorder got it.

The hawk's scream is apparently intended to lure small mammals out of hiding, to arouse their curiosity as to what misfortune might have befallen one of their own, much like humans are attracted to car crashes and fires.

But the hawk had no takers in this particular stretch of woods, no ambulance chasers. She followed the tree line down to the creek, then flew off to the south and out of sight. I decided to go into the woods and see what the hawk might have missed.

The bottomland swamp was soggy with recent rain. Water moved through the main stream, but the surrounding land was spongy and saturated. Greenbrier had been nibbled off by deer, whose prints were all over. There were numerous fallen trees, with trunks now rotted but root complexes full of forest life.

I stood by a fallen tree, leaned against a sweet gum, and waited. In a few minutes, the birds reappeared: a titmouse, chickadee, red-bellied woodpecker, yellow-rumped warbler, and then a flicker, which chased off the red-bellied woodpecker.

The root mass of the fallen pine stood more than six feet tall. I saw a brown blur in it and went to take a closer look. What a great little habitat, I noted—a miniature version of cliff dwellings. Beneath the root mass was a shallow puddle in what had been the root cavity of the live tree. I stood in the puddle and looked at the root mass. There were several species of fungi, numerous small openings, and perhaps a half dozen bird- or mouse-size holes worn smooth by heavy traffic. Wood shavings trailed from one. There was an empty

acorn shell, and live roots had been gnawed to expose the sweet sap.

The surface of the puddle in which I was standing was pocked by water droplets. It had begun to rain. I recorded another message for myself: "Waterproof boots."

I decided to follow the flow of the stream, which begins in the small town west of the farm and ends up in Finney Creek, which joins Burton's Bay and eventually the Atlantic Ocean. Streams such as these are called drains (pronounced "dreens"), and when they enter the salt marsh and become somewhat wider they are called guts. When a gut grows up it becomes a creek. And so goes the taxonomy of the seaside.

The drains, guts, and creeks are a lot like blood vessels in the human body. Some are large, some are tiny, yet all are linked, sharing a common vessel called the heart. The drains, guts, and creeks where I live on the Virginia coast begin as watershed drains, grow into substantial bodies of water, and eventually join the Atlantic Ocean, their great common vessel.

The kinship between the Atlantic Ocean and a watershed stream draining a farm or small town is difficult for me to grasp. The ocean is limitless and mysterious. It is cosmopolitan, reaching around the world to touch Spain, England, Scandinavia, Africa, India, encompassing thousands of islands great and small. This little stream, so modest and limited, seems an unlikely partner. It does not even have a name.

Once it leaves the town, the stream runs through woods and is out of view except for where it crosses under roads and winds through residential areas. Even after a rainy week it is only two feet wide, yet it is bordered by flat, boggy bottomland saturated with water.

The water in the stream was clear and fresh, mainly rainwater running slowly downslope from the town, farm fields, and woods drained by this particular watershed. I was tempted to taste it, but thought better of it. The health department has prohibited gathering shellfish in the creek fed by the stream because of fecal contamination, meaning that *E. coli* bacteria are being carried by the stream to the creek, making the clams and oysters living there dangerous to eat. The bacteria may have a human origin, emanating from inadequate septic systems in the nearby town, but increasing evidence points to animal contamination. The well-trod streamside is dotted with scat: marbly deer turds, shell-filled muskrat droppings, and loose brown middens filled with persimmon seeds. What opportunistic creatures raccoons and opossums are, eating their fill and then expanding the larder for future generations when they shit.

I rummaged through the game pocket of my hunting vest for the orange and ate it, spitting the seeds on streambed sand.

The stream is clearly the focal point of Bellevue's animal and bird population and is apparently enjoyed by all. On both sides the leaves were matted and the ground packed by heavy traffic. An empty oyster shell was surrounded by raccoon footprints. Deer had been drinking along a sandy edge, leaving their wedge-shaped prints in the damp earth. A titmouse bathed in the shallow water, shaking and fluffing its feathers.

From a distance the water appeared rusty, but the rust actually was orange algae growing on the bottom. Tiny filaments slow-danced in the current as the water left the farm and headed for the sea.

Here and there along the stream were small, sandy

beaches made of topsoil washed down with each heavy rain from an adjacent farm field. It's amazing how far topsoil can travel. The field is on the other side of the woods, at least a hundred yards away and still farther upstream. Yet down here in the woods, far removed, soil that once grew soybeans now forms a picnic beach for raccoons.

The little fans of topsoil are like growth rings in a tree. A band close to the field was washed down two years ago. One that empties into the creek proper is perhaps twenty-five years old; it left the field during a northeaster when Nixon was president and is just now making the trip of several miles to the deep part of the creek, and hence to the bay and the ocean.

The stream spiraled around sweet gum roots, cutting away the soil and leaving a hard bank of gray clay and twisted wood. Now and then I would come across a soda can or beer bottle. They were especially evident where the stream nears a farm field. Workers slaked their thirst with a cold one last July, then tossed the empties into the woods . . . out of sight, out of mind.

Strangely, the stream disappeared underground, falling with a pleasant splash into an opening perhaps two feet in diameter covered with white foam. From there it ran underground—I could hear the flow of water—and emerged again some twenty feet away. A lush growth of moss covered fallen trees and exposed roots.

I made a misstep and went in over my boot, falling forward and grasping a small sassafras tree. I pulled myself out and realized that the tree in front of me was a deer rub, its bark worn away by a buck scraping the velvet from his rack.

Finally the stream widened, though it was still shallow, and the vegetation changed. There were cattails, marsh elders,

brown remnants of pickerelweed. I surprised a pair of wood ducks and they surprised me. At close range, I could hear the muffled power of wings beating air. They rose from the water and in a second had cleared the thicket and were gone beyond the tree line.

Farther along, the *Spartina* grasses began to grow as the water became salty and widened to the size of a proper creek. *Spartina alterniflora,* a lush cordgrass, grows close to the water. In winter it is brown and lifeless, but in spring it will regain its vigor. Thick rhizomes embrace the muddy soil, hold it in a lacy grip. At the edge of the creek was a great blue heron, a stern-looking bird that paced the shallows like an impatient schoolmarm. The bird froze as a setter might, locking up on point as it spied a killifish among the brown leaf litter on the creekbottom. It struck with surprising speed, shook its great head side to side, flipped the minnow to a headfirst position, and then downed it with the dispatch of a shop owner ringing up a sale.

The water was tidal now, salty. The bottom was too soft to walk on—a soupy mixture of decaying plant matter, topsoil from the farm field, fine sand weathered to powder. If I looked at the mud with a magnifier, I could see the tiny grains, the bits of cellulose dropped by the rotting *Spartina* stems. Who knows what else is in there. Shellfish larvae, tiny plants called phytoplankton, bacteria, farm chemicals washed down with topsoil—all these are part of the soup.

Around the bend of the creek I could see the boats and houses at the town of Wachapreague, some three or four miles down the coast. From here the creek deepens, flowing seaward with the pulse of tides. The woods ends and there is only salt marsh, and then open bay. In the distance, beyond the crisp brown grasses of the marsh, I could see the ocean.

Fatwood

Last Sunday was a great day to search for fatwood. It was cold and windy, spitting snow. A northeast wind swept across Burton's Bay and dusted the gray furrows of Bellevue's cutover soybean fields. It stung our faces. But as soon as we stepped into the woods we were all right, comfortable in the shelter of the pine thicket.

Our supply of fatwood had dwindled through fall and early winter, and we needed to refill the box that sits on our back porch next to the firewood. A slender stick of fatwood contains about a century's worth of resins from the southern yellow pine, and it gets a fire going quicker than anything I've found.

I'll put two pieces of split cherry in the woodstove, drop a piece of fatwood between them, add a few sticks of dry pine, then reach under and put a match to the fatwood. It burns long and hot and soon has the cherry blazing away.

We could have bought fatwood—the outdoor catalogs offer genuine Georgia fatwood wrapped in neat bundles—but we prefer to collect our own and save our fatwood money for other things.

Besides, searching for fatwood is a pleasant way to spend a winter afternoon, especially when a hard wind is cutting across the field and snow is gathering in the soybean furrows.

In the woods it was quiet and still. We stood silently for a few minutes and took it all in. The birds, too, enjoyed the shelter of the woods. Tiny yellow-rumped warblers—their butter-yellow rumps flashing in the sun—flitted through the cedars and wax myrtles that line the edge. On the other side of the woodlot was Finney Creek, and now and then we could hear the raucous squawking of black ducks gathered in the lee.

Tom, from a very early age, has learned that all kinds of treasures can be found in the forest. Fatwood is one of his favorites. It is plentiful in these woods, which were logged perhaps two generations ago, and Tom takes great pleasure in finding more than Lynn and I do.

The pines in the woods at Bellevue are mature, and the fatwood we find comes from the previous generation of trees that were cut forty or fifty years ago. To find fatwood, we look for an ancient stump that has a vein of heartwood still remaining in its center. Although the circumference of the stump has rotted, the core can often be found intact, a slim marrow of weathered wood heavy and dense with resins. This gray core extends aboveground the height of the stump and underground for a foot or two. Give it a kick to loosen it up, then pull it out of the stump. If you're lucky, you'll have a vein of fatwood two or three feet long, enough for a month's worth of fatwood sticks.

We knock the dirt and rotten wood off the veins of fatwood, then bring them home and cut them into sticks with a

hatchet. It is remarkable to me that a pine tree long dead, long converted into lumber, can retain this sparkling residue of life.

Slice into the gray vein and you reveal a wonderfully rich concentration of resins and cellulose the color of topaz. It has the fragrance of turpentine, only sweeter. It's wonderful stuff, the essence of a pine tree that began life more than a century ago, concentrated here in a stump root reduced to the size of a person's arm.

Our fatwood isn't as neatly packaged as the bundles advertised as Georgia fatwood in the outdoor catalogs. Theirs is cut to length on a band saw; ours is chopped and split with a hatchet. We save the little chips and knots to restart a fire that has burned down.

The appeal of fatwood is not simply its ability to start a fire. The fire is but the single final step in the process of gathering, preparing, and using the wood. The good thing about fatwood trips is that they force you to get in the woods and look around. We always find some interesting things. On Sunday, for example, we came across a thicket of fox grape that some animal had been dining on. The thickest branches at ground level had been gnawed, as though some low-slung animal had found the bark very tasty. The vines were glistening with sap.

Then we found an owl pellet, which always is a nice treasure. Owls eat their prey whole, then regurgitate the undigestible parts. Find an owl pellet, and you can get a good idea of what the local owls have been dining on. We crumbled the pellet and found mainly fur and tiny bones. Apparently, this owl had been keeping Bellevue's population of field mice in check.

Peter Ling © 1996

And there are always birds. White-throated sparrows flitted through the undergrowth, and a yellow-rumped warbler took a higher perch in a gum tree. On the creek, enjoying the calm on the leeward side of the woods, were black ducks, green-winged teal, mergansers, mallards, yellowlegs, and a great blue heron. We would take breaks from gathering our fatwood to watch them through the binoculars.

By midafternoon we had collected all the fatwood we could carry, so we struck off across the field into the wind, arms laden with ancient wood. The snow swirled across the barren field and the wind stung our faces. Back home, we took the hatchet to the wood, cut off a healthy sliver, and in a few minutes had a roaring fire. It burned brightly and warmed us thoroughly.

A Blustery Day

Animals act strangely when the wind blows. Yesterday was sunny and blustery, with the temperature just above freezing—a good time for a walk in the woods. I drove down to Bellevue Farm, and in the front field two deer were standing in the lee of the woods. They looked at me with curiosity but made no move to leave. I stopped the truck, rolled down the window, and looked at them with the binoculars. They were chewing on winter wheat.

With hunting season not long past, these deer seemed remarkably nonchalant. Finally, the larger one raised its tail, sauntered into the woods, and the other followed.

A big red-tailed hawk zoomed in from over the treetops, head to the wind. It soared and veered off like a fighter plane, then circled, dove, and again headed into the wind and gained altitude. The bird clearly wasn't hunting, but instead seemed to be enjoying itself in the wind—diving, soaring, circling—hardly ever moving its broad wings.

Later I saw a turkey vulture do the same thing. From a

distance it looked like a northern harrier hunting field mice, but then I put the binoculars on it and realized it was a vulture. Again, the bird was not hunting, but seemed to be playing in the wind the way children enjoy the first snowfall of winter.

I decided to hike through the woods and along the creek edge to the headwaters, which would be sheltered and would have a lot of ducks. In the woods, I could hear the wind rip through the canopy of pines, but in the understory it was calm, and in pools of sunlight it was almost warm.

I heard birds in a pine thicket. A squirrel skittered off through the leaves. I made a pishing sound, did it again, and a yellow-rumped warbler landed in a bare oak less than ten feet from me. It was followed by a Carolina chickadee. I pished a few more times and a tufted titmouse appeared, and then a kinglet. More warblers came. The chickadee fussed at me.

Pishing is an old birdwatchers' trick. In the language of yellow-rumped warblers, the pishing sound means "fight, fight!" So all the other birds come to see what manner of excitement is taking place, and perhaps to aid in the defense of the community, should the need arise.

On the open creek, the water was frothy with little whitecaps. It was brown from recent rain, carrying a load of topsoil. No ducks there. I would have to go on to the headwaters.

On the bank were waste middens from raccoons and muskrats. There was deer scat. I had heard recently that much of the bacteria in local creeks is thought to come from wild animals. Here in the woods, exploring the creek shore, I can believe it. The creek is closed to shellfishing, and the animals may be the reason. I read recently that one raccoon bowel movement contains as much bacteria as one of a human, and the bacteria is slow to die. I imagined an ambitious new project for the state game department, a massive trapping program in which raccoons and muskrats would be captured and then fitted with Pampers. I'm not sure what they'd do with deer, maybe potty train them. Save an oyster—potty train a deer.

Walking through the woods on a windy day is a pleasure—you can hear the wind rip, see the trees sway, yet feel fairly comfortable in little islands of sunlight. I had only one problem. This old Barry Manilow hit, "Old Songs," kept going through my mind and I couldn't lose it. I don't especially like Barry Manilow's music, and I found the song irritating, like a guest who will not leave. I discovered I was walking in cadence with the tempo of the song, so I slowed down.

I walked to the head of the creek, Barry Manilow lyrics lingering like a case of hiccups. I decided to eat an orange.

An orange is the perfect hiking snack. It satisfies both hunger and thirst, gives you energy, and you have no bottles to return. I sliced mine into quarters, wiped the knife on my pants, and sucked the little orange sections from the rind. The orange had been in the game pocket of my jacket and was refreshingly cold.

I could hear green-winged teal in the shallow water in the lee of the woods. They sounded like spring peepers. I crawled on my belly through the woods and down a hill, and hid behind some myrtle bushes. Peering through the shrubs, I could see the ducks. Teal in the distance, black ducks within shotgun range, all with their heads underwater, feeding.

It's interesting how the wind makes animals act strangely.

Usually blacks would be very wary, away from shore, a lookout posted. I studied them with the binoculars, chewed the last of my orange, and hummed along with Barry Manilow.

In the winter woods, without its cover of leaves, it's easy to find tracks and trails. By this time of year they are well worn, like the potholed streets in town. I came across a good deer trail, worn almost into a trough. It ran along the crest of a hill, then downward to a bottomland swamp. I followed it there, to a place where deer had obviously been congregating.

On an impulse, I peed on their trail, marking it with what to them would be a puzzling and perhaps dangerous scent. I wondered what the deer would think when they came across it. Would they recognize it as human? I had never played a practical joke on a deer before.

I moved out for some distance, sat on the ground beneath a substantial oak tree, and waited for the deer. I gave it an hour, but no deer showed, and I began to suspect that they wouldn't be passing this way until dusk, which was still several hours off. And with the wind blowing, the deer might not even come at all. In blustery weather, animals often are unpredictable and act strangely. I stood up, stretched my legs, and made my way back to the truck.

Past Presence

On Bellevue Farm, human history lives in evidence found in the farm fields and woods. No one has lived here for more than fifty years, but past generations have left their marks, and they add mystery to my daily hikes. An arrowhead Tom found in a marsh-front field the other day is approximately six thousand years old, according to a guidebook we have. Everywhere there is evidence of past residents, reaching far back, well before the time of Christ. In the sandy farm fields we find stone tools, shards of pottery, and pipe stems, detritus from a time long gone.

I go down to the farm in early summer, after the farmer has plowed the fields, after spring rains have washed the soil from rocks and pottery. It's a good time to walk the fields, because they are barren and open. The woods by now have become thick with honeysuckle and sassafras. The deciduous trees have leafed out, making it virtually impossible to see birds. The ticks and chiggers are plentiful; mosquitoes bloom in great clouds as the larvae mature in shallow rain puddles.

So I go in the woods less often and instead listen from the edge for the trill of pine warblers and look for human detritus scattered about the barren ground.

Here on the coast, rocks are rare finds, and most were brought to the area for a purpose—stone tools, ship ballast, construction material—so when I find a rock, I try to determine its purpose. Last week I found a rock in the shape of an equilateral triangle, about four inches per side and one inch thick. I picked it up, wiped away the soil, and began handling it. I soon found slight depressions on the top edge for the right index finger and along the side for the thumb. Later, after I had washed the rock, I could see that these depressions had been darkened by the oil of human skin, and the bottom edge of the tool had been polished by use.

Clearly, the triangular rock had been used as a tool, but for what purpose? A rather blunt scraper, perhaps, or a tool for crushing nuts and grain? Our books on American Indians of the region provided no clues, but evidence indicates that the earliest residents were hunter-gatherers rather than planters, so our tool was most likely used to process skins.

Disappointingly little is known about the American Indians of the Eastern Shore. The first written accounts begin in 1608, when Captain John Smith explored the Chesapeake region from his base at Jamestown. He noted that there were two major tribes on what is now the Virginia portion of the Eastern Shore: the Accomacs and the Occohannocks, both of which spoke the language of the Powhatans and traded with them. But there is scant evidence from years prior to contact with Europeans, and Smith likely had no knowledge at all of the smaller Eastern Shore groups that populated seaside areas such as Bellevue Farm.

Evidence of human activity on Bellevue Farm is subtle,

especially for untrained eyes such as my own. I walk along and kick at stones, sometimes finding shards of glazed pottery, but more often colorful bits of more contemporary dinnerware.

The most obvious links with Bellevue's human history are the cemetery and the old house site where several generations of the Parramore family lived. Not much is left. The old home, Bellevue Plantation, was abandoned in the 1940s and was eventually dismantled for its heart pine lumber. What is left is the crumbling brick foundation, most of which has caved in. Honeysuckle winds through the bricks, virtually hiding them for most of the year. Trees grow thirty or forty feet tall where the Parramores once entertained guests. Not long ago I found the old well that provided water for the plantation house; it had been filled with brick rubble, no doubt to prevent accidents. In a thick wooded area east of the house, near the salt marsh, was the Parramore garbage dump; I have found many old bottles here.

Just north of the house was the cook kitchen. The huge old chimney is still standing, and with it the original fireplace where the Parramores' meals were prepared. It is home now for a family of raccoons.

About one hundred yards west of the house site is the family cemetery, where several generations of Parramores are buried. Gnarled old trees surround the graveyard, and these too have become homes to raccoons. The gravestones of Colonel William and Sarah Parramore are still standing, but with a noticeable lean. Other graves were covered with flat marble slabs engraved with information about the occupants. Most of the slabs have been broken, most likely by vandals hoping to find something of value beneath. We have restored them as well as we can, leveling the land and pressing the heavy chunks back together along their fault lines. We have

cleaned the marble gravestones with bleach and detergent, applied with a stiff brush, until they became white again and the inscriptions legible.

Walking the farm, I think about the Parramores and their lives at Bellevue. By today's standards, the farm is remote, well off the beaten path. The county road that provides access is seldom traveled, with the exception of the farmer, the few neighbors, and teenagers looking for a secluded place to park.

For the Parramores, their avenue of commerce and communication would have been more often by water than the county road. Farm products were shipped from the plantation dock, and various necessities, as well as frequent visitors, would have come by water. If anything, given the popularity of boat traffic two hundred years ago, the farm would have been considered less remote than it is today. The Parramores were community leaders, they lived in a fine home, and they must have entertained lavishly and often.

Whereas now the business of raccoons and great horned owls occupies the evenings at Bellevue, many years ago the business would have dealt with a struggling young country in the process of asserting its independence.

The first Parramores came to America as indentured servants, but by the time of the Revolution they were among the leaders of the growing Virginia colony. John Parramore arrived in 1622 as a seventeen-year-old servant, but by the early 1640s he had an indentured servant of his own.

The Parramore connection with Bellevue Farm came by marriage. Thomas Parramore, a grandson of John, married the widow Joanna Custis Hope, who had inherited Bellevue Farm and Parramore Island from her grandfather. Thomas outlived Joanna, and when he died he bequeathed the property to his son William. The plantation home whose ruins remain in evidence was built in 1818 by Thomas Parramore, son of William. It replaced an older and more modest dwelling occupied by William and his wife, Sarah.

I can vaguely recall, as a small child, exploring the abandoned plantation house with my father. I remember very little about it, only a narrow attic hallway that became in my mind a secret passage, and a hatch of some sort on the roof, which afforded a splendid view of the seaside marshes, barrier islands, and on the horizon, the ocean.

So as I walk the fields of Bellevue I also dredge up the detritus of my own life, kicking at stones, trying to find some switch that will help me illuminate darkened corners of my memory.

A Reverence for Rocks

When I walk the fields at Bellevue Farm, my eyes are on the ground directly ahead of me. I walk slowly and somewhat slumped, with a halting gait. If someone were to drive by on the county road and see me, their impression would be that I am a very old man, a tired and infirm man who is enjoying one of his last drinks of sunshine.

But I am neither old nor infirm, nor am I drinking in the sunshine. I am looking for rocks, and my mind is a thousand miles away and on many different things. I am looking for Indian rocks—stone tools and weapons—and as my eyes scan the ground, my thoughts leap from here to there. Looking for Indian rocks is an exercise in dividing my brain activity into two separate functions. My eyes watch the ground, and my brain quickly discriminates and catalogs: pebble, pebble, pebble, pottery, possible Indian rock. Meanwhile, another part of my brain is racing away in a separate direction, turning inward instead of outward. I compose sentences for writing projects. I think about politics and money. I plan trips. I have erotic fantasies.

These thoughts go on uninterrupted until an alarm sounds, the two brains merge, and I realize that my foot is kicking at a possible spear point or scraper.

I am not good at finding Indian rocks, because my inward thoughts sometimes become so intense that they override the alarm system. But that is the very reason I search for stone tools—so that I can walk the fields slowly and aimlessly, allowing my mind to wander.

Yesterday Lynn and Tom and I were walking along the top of an old earthen dike built to hold dredge spoil. Tom, who was third in line, found a beautiful spear point, which Lynn and I had both nearly stepped on. At age nine, he seems to have a knack for finding Indian rocks, and I think the reason is that he's not looking for them. When he found the spear point he was tired and angry, in one of his rare obstinate moods. He was swinging a stick back and forth, hitting little cedar trees, when his eyes happened upon the spear point. Two weeks ago, when we were doing the Christmas bird count, Tom was throwing dirt clods along the edge of the farm field when he picked up a nice arrowhead.

Here on the Virginia coast we have a certain reverence for rocks, and the reason is that we have very few native stones. By the time rocks reach the coast they are ground down and weathered to sand, fragments of rocks, fragments of mountains. So to find a rock is in many instances akin to finding an archaeological treasure. In a farm field, a rock is a symbol of life.

I once found a stone ax in one of Bellevue's marsh-front fields. I was walking across the field in my usual manner, when I saw the nub of a rock in the newly plowed land. I

kicked at it and the alarm sounded. The two sides of my brain converged. It was a beautiful little ax head, about four inches long by two inches wide. The blade was remarkably sharp, and though it was a fairly coarse rock, it had been worn smooth by use. The blunt end was flattened and hammerlike. What I had was a Stone Age version of the Boy Scout ax, an ancient prototype. It excited the imagination. I brushed the sand away, rubbed the rock against my pants, and felt the smooth sharpness and symmetry some talented toolmaker had achieved. It seemed remarkable that someone had used this tool at this spot possibly thousands of years ago, before the arrival of Europeans and Africans, long before this field had been cultivated for the first time. And now I, in the here and now, and he, the Indian who once hunted here, were linked by a smooth rock. He was the last to touch this rock, many, many years ago, and now I hold it in my hand. In the rock I can feel our kinship.

In a land where there are few native rocks, stones have come to represent history. I have in my garden rocks that were used as ballast stones on my great-grandfather's sailing schooner. Not long after I began hiking on Bellevue Farm, I found the ballast stones used in one of Colonel William Parramore's ships. They were in a hedgerow covered with honeysuckle and briers and would have been invisible in most months except January and February. It was hard to walk in there, but it was a spot in the hedgerow I had not yet seen and so I was determined to go there. I stumbled over the stones by accident as I tore my way through the greenbrier.

The Parramore stones were dark, and each weighed about thirty pounds. There was a whole pile of them. They were near the old house site and some distance from water, which was puzzling. But a decent stream ran through the hedgerow, and it takes a small leap of imagination to make this stream into a navigable waterway two hundred years ago, when boats would have come inland to load farm produce, and in doing so off-load their ballast.

When the Indians hunted these woods and marshes, gathering oysters and clams, trade was established with the Powhatans of the western shore and the tribes that preceded them. The hardshell clam of the coast, *Mercenaria mercenaria,* was so named because the shells were used as money. Disk-shaped tribute beads called roanoke were made from hardshell clams and mussels, and these were highly regarded by western tribes. Eastern Shore Indians traded roanoke to the Powhatans, but what they received in return is uncertain;

stone tools and other implements likely were a part of the bargain, given the scarcity of native rock. The stone ax I found, or Tom's spear point, might have come from the Blue Ridge mountains, or perhaps from the north, the Adirondacks, the product of a transaction that took place long ago.

Did some local hunter swap a few polished clamshells to a western tribesman for this beautiful ax? I can imagine his delight at having turned such a deal. "Six clamshells—what a steal!" he'd tell himself. "First I feast on the meat of the clam, and then I swap the empty shells for this wonderful tool. What a shrewd trader I am."

And on the other side of the transaction, the dealers in stone tools making their way back west would be elbowing each other in the ribs and making jokes about the dumb coastal Indian who had given up six glistening shells for a single crude rock. "When we get back to Powhatan with these clamshells, we'll be heroes," they'd boast.

The commerce between the stone dealers and the shell traders is by no means limited to the ancient tribes. Here on the Virginia coast, gift shops are filled with local seashells and handcrafts made of shells. When tourists visit from the mountains, they pay a lot of money for these trinkets, and they scour the beaches for whelks and sun-bleached clamshells, which they take home and display with pride in their flower gardens.

Likewise, when our family goes to the Blue Ridge, we scout the streambeds for glistening rocks, and we drag them to the car and wedge them between the suitcases in the trunk. At home, they are displayed with pride in our flower garden.

In college I took a geology course, which I barely passed. Spending a semester studying rocks sounded fascinating, but I discovered that my appreciation for rocks was more sensual

than scientific. I didn't care whether a rock was igneous or metamorphic; I cared only about its color, texture, and shape.

My reverence for rocks is possibly genetic. My great-aunt Marceline, whom everyone called Tootsie—the woman who raised my mother and who thus became ipso facto my grandmother—collected thousands of rocks in her ninety-some years. Her husband was in the produce business, and when he would send a truck loaded with potatoes to a market west of the fall line, he would always instruct the driver to bring home some rocks on the return trip.

So Tootsie became the only person in our town to have a rock fence around her house. She also built rock gardens, rock birdbaths, and rock ponds for turtles and goldfish. When I was little I would stand on the edge of the goldfish pond and scatter dry oatmeal over the water, and the fish would rise slowly, glowing in the thick green water, and nibble the oats. Tootsie built a rock "sun porch" onto the turtle pond, and on warm spring days after school we would go quietly to the pond and watch the diamondbacks and painted turtles sun themselves.

Although Tootsie built things with her rocks, they meant far more to her than mere construction material. She was a woman of great energy and creativity, and she could look at the rocks and find the shapes of familiar things: a car, a house, a face. She saved the most richly colored and shapely rocks for special places, such as the small rock garden near her front door, or for the rock gateposts at the front of the house. Like me, she didn't know igneous from metamorphic, but she sensed that rocks had a certain link with human life.

Tootsie never tired of finding building projects that involved rocks. Her pièce de résistance was the stone fence that surrounded her home, built after years of collecting, after hundreds of shipments of potatoes and cucumbers. It was a

Peter King © 1996

friendly fence, low and flat-topped, built not to keep people out but to entertain, to amuse. We children would climb on it and walk along its ridge, holding our arms out tightrope fashion, testing our balance. Tootsie would watch us from her front porch, happy that we were sharing her delight.

We don't have enough rocks yet to build a fence. Our rocks have more modest duties, such as protecting the rosebush from the dogs, or serving as a flower border. But after a few more vacations to the Blue Ridge, I figure we should have the beginnings of a goldfish pond. Tootsie, I think, would be pleased.

Zen Birding

It has become a ritual in our family to spend a day of our Christmas holiday counting birds. We have done this for several years now—Lynn, Tom, and I. Each year we count the birds on Bellevue Farm, walking the hedgerows to find white-throated sparrows and scanning the bay for brant and mergansers. We are among thousands of people nationwide who take part in the annual Audubon Christmas Bird Count, and the results, compiled year after year, give ornithologists an idea of how the populations of various species are faring.

In truth, I have my misgivings about the scientific reliability of data turned in by thousands of birdwatchers running around the countryside with their binoculars and field guides one day a year. Most of the counters are probably like us. We do it because we enjoy it, not because we are under the illusion we are contributing to scientific inquiry. It makes us feel good.

Bellevue Farm supports a remarkable diversity of bird life. We regularly count sixty or more species, and I suspect that if we really tried we could find more. Our count begins at dawn, and usually there are flocks of Canada geese and greater snow geese grazing on winter wheat in the farm fields. We rouse them and make a count as they are silhouetted against the rising sun.

On Burton's Bay there always are rafts of brant. If the winter has come early and harsh, there will be thousands; if it has been mild, a few hundred. There will be greater yellowlegs and great blue herons on the shoreline, clapper rails in the marshes, and loons and red-breasted mergansers in the channel of Finney Creek. When the tide ebbs, the exposed flats will have black-bellied plovers, dunlins, sanderlings, and various other difficult-to-identify birds we lump together under "peep species."

The hedgerows of Bellevue Farm hold the greatest number of birds. There is something in the mindset of modern farming that detests a hedgerow. They are mowed and sprayed with herbicides, plowed to their margins, and set upon with chain saws until there is nothing left but the drainage ditch that the vegetation once concealed. And this is a shame, because hedgerows are wonderful places, full of animals, birds, and interesting plants. Those on Bellevue Farm are lush, thanks to a farmer who shares our appreciation for them.

Some hedgerows have very old trees. One particular hedgerow across from the old house site has a giant sycamore, a lovely tree whose white bark stands beautifully stark against a gray winter sky. This tree's immediate ancestors were part of the farm when William Parramore lived here. This sycamore grew from stock produced when Virginia was a colony, when Colonel William was fighting the redcoats.

Beneath the old sycamore are sassafras, sweet gum, cedar,

and oak trees. There are wax myrtles, sumacs, and persimmon trees, honeysuckle, poison ivy, Virginia creeper, and greenbrier. A twisted wild cherry tree with a hollow core holds a family of raccoons. A fox has a den in a streambank. High overhead, canoe-shaped seed pods of trumpet vine clatter together in the breeze. Goldfinches have them staked out; they flutter over them hungrily and deftly pick tiny seeds from the pods.

On the bird count, Lynn and Tom walked on one side of the hedgerow and I walked on the other, herding the birds along in front of us and, when the hedgerow ended, into view. I used my little microcassette recorder to take notes because it's difficult to count birds and add numbers at the same time. If I saw a bird I couldn't identify, I would describe it on tape and look it up later.

When I am alone, I'll walk into a hedgerow and sit quietly for some time. Most hedgerows on Bellevue Farm have drainage ditches running through them. If the ditch is dry, I'll walk down it and sit on its edge and try to see and hear as much as I possibly can. This is passive birding, becoming an unmoving observer, a sponge that soaks up all it comes in contact with. Birding with Lynn and Tom is by nature active birding; we hike and we herd and we count, and by day's end we are weary. After an afternoon of passive birding I am renewed and energized, rich with new sights and sounds.

Passive birding is Zenlike in that it is a contemplative act, one that encourages you to look inward as well as to sensitize yourself to the world outside yourself. And, of course, passive birding, Zen birding, deals with more than birds. It involves observation, stillness, and the eventual development of a mental state that purges extraneous thoughts.

When I am alone on Bellevue Farm, I sometimes will walk the field road at a fast pace, or perhaps jog across the fields and through the woods down to Channel Point. When my body is tired, I will go into the woods or a hedgerow and sit down. I find that a certain degree of physical exhaustion helps me come to the proper mental state for Zen birding. I no longer feel the need to move around, my muscles are warm, my head is clear. I can sit and watch the woods, seeing not only the birds that have come to accept my presence, but also the gnarled roots of cherry trees in the ditchbank, the twisting threads of honeysuckle, the drama of a Cooper's hawk attacking a quail. The woods become my community, and I get to know them as well as the neighborhood where I grew up. The twisted cedar becomes a landmark, the white-throated sparrows daily acquaintances. I live here.

Thinking of the hedgerow as my community makes me a better birder, because I know who lives where. The birds on the ground ahead of me, feeding in the grassy field edge, are palm warblers. I know they are palm warblers even before I can see their yellow underparts, see them bob their tails as they forage along in the grass. Juncos and some sparrows feed on the ground, too, but they don't act quite like palm warblers.

In the hedgerow are different strata of bird communities. Dark-eyed juncos live on the bottom floor in tight little ethnic neighborhoods, as do bobwhite quail. Rufous-sided towhees are there too, but are solitary workers. White-throated and song sparrows and gray catbirds occupy the next floor, followed by northern cardinals, Carolina chickadees, and tufted titmice. Yellow-rumped warblers live on the mid to top floors.

Even beyond the hedgerow community, birds have their own particular niches. Red-tailed hawks, bald eagles, and vultures soar high overhead on thermals. Hawks, eagles, and black vultures hunt with their eyes, and the red-tailed augments its efforts with sound effects, a piercing scream that sounds like a small mammal in distress. The turkey vulture, unlike the black vulture, locates its meals by sense of smell. Northern harriers fly low over the farm fields and marsh, searching for mice. American kestrels perch on trees, fences, and power lines, waiting for a small mammal or large insect to show itself. Sharp-shinned and Cooper's hawks hunt the hedgerow, darting into thickets to grasp a warbler or sparrow.

On the water, diving ducks hunt in the channel of Finney Creek, while black ducks, wigeon, mallards, and other surface-feeding ducks gather in the shallow waters of the freshet where the tidal creek joins the land.

Over time, I've developed something of a mental map of Bellevue Farm, a diagram that assigns the various residents their own particular quarters, like a layout of an apartment building. This is an oversimplification, of course, not taking into account the usual moving about of wild things or the tremendous number of migrant songbirds that move through the farm in spring and fall. But it helps on the occasion of events such as the Christmas bird count, when we do our annual census of the neighborhood.

The value of the bird count, it seems to me, is not the information it feeds to computer databanks regarding bird populations, but the fact that it encourages people like us to get out on the farm for a day, to get into the hedgerows and woods, and to discover what a remarkably diverse and rich world we live in. And there is the hope that we will return

Peter King ©1996

more often, perhaps alone, and spend quiet hours in the community of the hedgerow, not to count and to compile lists, but simply to sit on a ditchbank and become part of the woods.

Canoeing

Over the years, I've managed to collect numerous small boats, each of which has its own character and purpose. At one end of the spectrum, there is the fishing boat, a twenty-three-foot C-Hawk center console model that gets us out to the open water, where we fish for gray trout, croakers, striped bass, and anything else that is willing. And then there is the little Old Town Pack, a twelve-foot, one-person canoe made of ABS Royalex, a rugged, lightweight plastic compound. The boat weighs slightly more than thirty pounds, so I can throw it over one shoulder, pick up the paddles, and hike through the woods to some remote backwater to do my exploring.

As I mentioned, each boat has its own character and purpose, and so it is with these two. The family couldn't go bottom fishing in the middle of the Chesapeake Bay in the Pack, and we couldn't explore the headwaters of Finney Creek in the C-Hawk.

While I have spent many enjoyable hours in each boat, I have to admit that I like the smaller one better. Large boats are necessary for safety reasons in open water, but I enjoy putzing around in remote creek heads where the less boat you have the better life is. At thirty pounds, the Pack is not much boat.

A small boat propelled on one's own is a personal craft that allows access to any number of sensory elements. Bird songs are not overpowered by the noise of an outboard motor. You can feel the insistent urging of the tide and enjoy the aroma of marsh essence rather than combusted fossil fuel.

Though I enjoy fishing in the big boat, I resent the way it reduces my role in the relationship between person and setting. I am dependent upon a 150-horsepower motor to get me out and back. I know nothing about motors, other than to keep the gas tank full and to turn the switch key. I don't like being at the mercy of mechanical things.

The big boat, because it costs a lot of money, triggers the confiscatory reflex of various levels of government, which I also resent. When I bought it, I had to pay a watercraft tax to the state, plus I had to register it and license it, and I have to renew the license each year. I had to pay titling tax on the trailer and license it, and I also have to renew that license each year. I had to register the boat with my county government, and I have to pay them so much each year in personal property taxes. I had to buy certain items of mandatory safety equipment—life jackets, signaling devices, a fire extinguisher, and so on—which cost a lot of money. I bought a VHS radio to call for help in the event the outboard motor broke, and I have to pay the federal government a tax on that. I enjoy fishing, but to do so I must pay the state government for the privilege, and I must abide by regulations that have become increasingly complex. So my boat is licensed, my trailer is

Peter King ©1986

licensed, my radio is licensed, and I am licensed. This is what the outdoor experience has come to.

The little canoe, however, cost less than three hundred dollars, and the various governments that tax and regulate our lives could not care less about it, which is one of the reasons I like it. It is simple, clean, responsive, and undemanding. It sits in the backyard under the pin oak, waiting patiently for someone to come along with a paddle and a PFD (personal flotation device) and a willingness to explore.

In the summer months, the canoe is my vehicle for getting around Bellevue Farm. The woods are thick with honeysuckle; mosquitoes, ticks, and chiggers are on the attack. The canoe, however, gets me where I want to go. I can still explore the woods and marshes, but I do it from the water.

It is late June and I have been watching for a pair of bald eagles that nest each spring in a grove of tall pines on the shores of Finney Creek. Yesterday I went out to look for them in the canoe, paddling upstream with the incoming tide. I found the female bird first, along the northern shore, where she apparently had been feeding in the salt marsh. She ascended as I drew near, cleared the tree line, banked southward across the creek, and headed for the nesting area.

She landed on a limb high in a pine, and then I saw her mate, a smaller mature bird with white head and tail. I paddled a little farther and then saw a dark bird in the pine canopy, which I took at first to be a vulture. But as I came closer, I realized the bird was too large to be a vulture, and when I put the binoculars on it and saw the head, I realized it was an immature bald eagle, the offspring of the pair I had just passed. The nest was just a few feet away in the thick canopy of pines.

Peter King ©1996

Eagles nest early in the spring, and this young bird was probably the pair's only fledgling. It did not fly and I kept my distance, not wanting to spook it into a premature attempt at flight. If the eagles had nested in early March and the eggs hatched in early April, this bird would have been ready for flight. I left it and paddled toward the headwaters, and when I returned it was in the same nest tree.

When I'm paddling in deep water, I wear a Coast Guard approved PFD because I'm not a good swimmer. But when I reach the upper creek, where the water spreads itself thin over the flats, the PFD comes off. It was hot yesterday, and by the time I had reached the head of Finney Creek, my shirt was drenched with sweat. I pulled it off, draped it over the gunwale to dry, and drank a Dr. Pepper.

I customized this little canoe to fit my needs. I made a shelf from a piece of one-by-twelve pine to hold binoculars, microcassette recorder, notepad, drinks, and other items. I cut the pine to follow the curves of the gunwales and attached two wooden clips to the bottom. These fasten over the center thwart, holding the shelf in place. It is my floating office.

I use both single-blade and double-blade paddles. The double-blade is for open water and for traveling in relatively straight lines. When I reach the meandering creeks and guts of the upper marsh, I put it away and use the single-blade to maneuver around the bends.

The woven canoe seat, though comfortable, becomes tiring after an hour or so of paddling, so I change positions often and carry a cushion to kneel on. You can generate more power when paddling from a kneeling position because the large muscles of your legs come into play.

Water drips into the canoe from the paddles and collects in the bottom. Anything that's in the bottom of the canoe gets soaked. So I carry a sponge to sop up water and try to keep things as dry as possible. In the winter I tie pieces of rubber tubing around the shafts of the double paddle just above the blades. These encourage the water to drip outside the canoe instead of running down the shaft and dripping in my lap.

It occurred to me yesterday that canoeing in the upper marsh in summer is very similar to sitting quietly in a hedgerow in winter, an extension of Zen birding. I paddled hard from the put-in, worked up a sweat, got the pulse going. By the time I reached the upper marsh, my shoulders were tired, the tendon in my elbow ached, my butt was sore. I let the canoe cruise with the breeze and lay back against the gunwales as the boat drifted into a stand of cordgrass and wedged itself in a flooded thicket.

My arrival set off a squadron of tiny white flies that had gathered on the stalks of grass. They stormed the canoe for a few minutes and then fell silent again, returning to whatever business they were conducting on the cordgrass.

I stretched my feet out under the shelf, sat on the cushion in the bottom of the boat, and leaned against the edge of the seat. It was a thoroughly comfortable position, and it felt good to stretch my legs. I sipped the tepid Dr. Pepper and then fell quiet, as I do in winter in the hedgerows.

The hot sun felt good against my shoulders. The marsh was humid, and sweat trickled down my chest and collected on my belly. I soaked the sponge in water and drizzled it over my head, and then lay back to see what I could see.

First, there were egrets, a group of four snowys—small, plumed birds with black bills and yellow feet, looking as though they had been wading in a shallow tub of paint. They foraged for small fish along the marsh edge, and then flew off. They roost here in the upper marsh, and now and then I come across roosting trees, where the underbrush is white-washed with the birds' pungent waste.

Birds flitted about in the woods edge. From here in the creek, I explore the same edges and hedgerows I do in winter, but from the water side instead of land. I heard a northern cardinal, and then saw the flame-red male bird high in a myrtle thicket. I joked to myself that the birds are called northern cardinals because of their accent. "Is it da boid? Is it da boid? Is it da boid?" they ask.

I heard a loud squeak, which woke me up, and turned to see a green heron flying off across the creek. Then I heard a clapper rail, another marsh bird with a pneumatic voice, and saw blue jays doing battle in a pine thicket. A great blue heron, in all its dignity and splendor, waded languidly in a shallow gut, awaiting the passage of a school of minnows. And I awaited the imminent turn of the tide. The little boat rocked slightly as I moved, as the breeze played against it. I felt safe and comfortable lying in the bottom of the boat. It was womblike. I was ballast.

When the tide began to ebb, I would sit up, take the paddle, and make my way back to where I had launched, the trip made easier by following the current. But for now the tide was just turning, and I was comfortable and in absolutely no hurry to go anywhere.

Walking on Cheese

Here is my itinerary: I will park the truck near the old cemetery, read again the gravestone inscriptions, and then explore for the thousandth time the Parramore house site. Ready for a long walk, I will begin south of the house lot and follow the hedgerows along the field and shoreline, all the way down to the woods where the lane to Channel Point begins. I will walk down the lane to the point, and there I will sit on a cushion of salt-meadow hay and eat an orange and watch the buffleheads and mergansers dive for fish on Finney Creek. That will be the halfway mark.

Coming back, I will walk on the outside of the wooded peninsula along the high marsh, which is one of my favorite places on Bellevue Farm. Walking on the high marsh is like walking on cheese. It is moist and springy, and though it feels tenuous at first, it is altogether solid, packed with plant material, sand, and mud, perforated by thousands of holes excavated by fiddler crabs. Picture a thick sandy slab of Swiss cheese. This is what I will walk on.

It is winter, a glorious season for a walk in the marsh. It began snowing this morning at dawn, and after two fitful hours of attempting work, I gave up and drove down to the farm, mentally organizing my itinerary along the way. Snow was gathering around the Parramore gravestones; it collected in the barren furrows of the soybean field. Here on the coast, we get few snows. They are not to be wasted.

Upon arriving at the farm, I decided to alter my itinerary and go straightaway to the marsh, where the snow would hang like billowing cheesecloth over Burton's Bay and make the islands in the distance disappear. I pulled on a hooded sweatshirt, and over that I wore a waxed cotton jacket I had bought on a trip to England. It is a wonderful jacket, waterproof yet breathable, with lots of pockets, including a large game bag in the back. Two hand-warmer pockets are lined with moleskin. The British know how to make a jacket.

In the marsh it was remarkably still, and the white sky closed around me until I could not tell where the bay began and the sky ended. I was confined by snow, held in a private world where, after walking for twenty minutes, I could not tell where I had come from or where I was going.

In the quiet, snow rattled off the shoulders of my jacket, and I could hear it settling into the brittle spent shards of last season's cordgrass. I stopped to take it all in. I was in the upper marsh, where salt-marsh cordgrass *(Spartina alterniflora),* which grows in profusion along the channel edges, is joined by salt-meadow hay *(S. patens),* salt grass *(Distichlis spicata),* and black needlerush *(Juncus roemeranianus).* It is a wonderful landscape, especially in winter, especially in snow. Though the variety of plants is limited in this salty environment, they complement each other perfectly, creating a minimalist interpretation of botany as art. Salt-meadow hay lies in soft cowlicks, tumps of fine grass bending gracefully in pliant curves. Black needlerush is rigid and erect, and in winter its shafts turn nearly black. Those of salt-meadow hay become the color of ginger and at times, when the late-day sun is low on the horizon, can shimmer like gold.

Snow was gathering in the folds of salt-meadow hay and clung to individual shafts of grass, slowly bending them over. I walked on to where the upper marsh joins the fastland. I jumped up and down and could feel the packed earth tremble slightly. Beneath the layer of mud, pockmarked by the tunnels of fiddler crabs, was a layer of peat, all that remained of ancient marshes. It is the peat that gives the high marsh its cheeselike quality.

In the narrow zone where salt marsh joins fastland, the botanical list expands markedly. On slightly higher ground are sea lavender *(Limonium carolinianum),* sea oxeye *(Borrichia frutescens),* and switchgrass *(Panicum virgatum).* In the transition zone, where the high marsh meets the pine woods, grow marsh elder *(Iva frutescens),* groundsel tree *(Baccharis halimifolia),* wax myrtle *(Myrica cerifera),* and juniper *(Juniperus virginiana).* Underfoot, there are tubular little plants called saltwort, or *Salicornia.*

These plants determine the character of the landscape, and they change with the seasons and with the weather. The marsh is lush and fecund during summer. Sea oxeye has a brilliant yellow blossom, which attracts bees and butterflies. Sea lavender provides a soft purple background, with countless tiny flowers. Saltwort is green in summer, and like a maple tree in fall it turns a deep crimson.

But the marsh is at its best in winter, with the artful grasses, the heaviness of the sky, the harshness of the landscape that underscores its wildness. Northern harriers hunt

the high ground. Brant gather in the shallow bays. Foxes leave footprints in the snow . . . and occasionally the blood spilled from an early morning meal.

The plants of the marsh gain drama in winter. Sea oxeye, with its showy yellow flowers and succulent green leaves in summer, puts on its austere costume in winter. Spiky brown seedheads will remain on the plant until spring. Even sea lavender, which seems so dainty in summer, becomes severe, with small seedpods against a brown, wirelike filigree.

These marsh plants, when seen against a background of green cedar, with its thick clusters of blue berries, and holly, with its red berries, provide an appropriate winter counterpoint in color and design. The evergreens of the woods—the cedars, hollies, and pines—still appear dynamic, full of vitality. Flocks of cedar waxwings and finches settle in the tops of the trees, feeding on berries. The harsher the weather gets, the busier the neighborhood.

I enjoy the marsh in winter because it seems wilder, its beauty more subtle. The marsh is sienna against a background of evergreen, and the few accents of color—the blue and red berries, the yellow tail stripes of the cedar waxwings—are all the more emphatic. Birds feed with a sense of urgency, and whereas summer is fecund and fruitful, a time of growth, winter is a season of drama. It is *Macbeth* compared with *A Midsummer Night's Dream.*

I walked to Channel Point by way of the high marsh, then sat on a cedar stump and ate my orange. At my feet was a wrack line of decaying *Spartina,* intermixed with an eclectic assortment of shells, bottles, bones, driftwood, and crab pot floats, all of which had been delivered by the latest high tide. I kicked through the grass searching for treasure. You never know what you're going to find.

Recently I found the bottom portion of a huge old oar, the kind they once used in the surf boats at the lifesaving stations on the barrier islands. It was well up in the high marsh, wedged under some groundsel bushes, and apparently had been there for a long time. It was weathered and split, but there was no question as to what it was. I brought it home and hung it in my office.

Lynn's tastes run to the marsh plants, and in winter she snips off pieces of the dormant ones—sea oxeye, sea lavender, needlerush—and combines them with greenery to make flower arrangements and wreaths.

Tom is fond of turtle shells, and his bedroom looks like a biologist's specimen closet. There are shells and bones, rocks, egg casings, bottles, floats—all treasures gleaned from the upper marsh, deposited in a wrack line by high tides.

The upper marsh of Bellevue is unique to the mid-Atlantic in that one can stand upon it and see nothing but marsh from horizon to horizon. There are no roads, no signs, no interpretive kiosks, no houses, only an abandoned oyster watch house in the bay and, far in the distance, the outline of a few summer homes on Cedar Island.

What this means, I suspect, is that I enjoy this particular place not just for the plants, the animals, and the birds, but because I can enjoy them in the context of a wilderness setting. I can find the same plants and animals in parks, refuges, and other places, often with guides or booklets to help explain them to me, but that, it seems to me, devalues the experience.

It is like hearing the roar of a lion. If you hear the roar in a zoo, it is an entertaining event. But if you hear it while hiking the African bush, where there are no fences, it is not simply entertaining, but memorable.

I finished my orange and began the walk back to the truck on the wooded lane. The ground was covered with snow, which bent the pine boughs and cedars until they closed overhead, creating a tunnel of white. Already there was the track of a fox, and its blurred confluence with the track of a rabbit indicated a recent skirmish. Juncos foraged in leaf litter beneath a cedar.

The snow, in twenty-four hours, would be gone, or at least reduced to a muddy mess. I wanted to take it all in while I could—the way it clung to the trees, the quiet sound of snow settling upon snow, the rustling of birds, the quick violence of the fox, the sting of ice upon my bare cheeks, the isolation as the snow closed around me and covered my past and future.

I walked down the wooded lane and headed west along the field edge, and then saw the fresh prints of deer where the green remnants of winter wheat stood out in the lee of the woods. I wondered about the animals. Would they find the snow a burden, a threat to their dwindling food supplies? Or would they delight in it as I did? I, of course, had a hot wood fire awaiting me at home, and there was leftover clam chowder and cornbread for my lunch. I could afford to be smug about snow.

I walked with my head down, bent against a sudden breeze that piled the snow in drifts against the woods. I entered the woods. Snow covered the forest floor, clung to leaves and branches. The rough gray forms of wild cherry trees stood out against the white background in a wonderful mosaic. Limbs twisted against each other, growing at odd angles I had not noticed before. In dense thickets such as this, trees have to be opportunists, reaching where they can for sunlight, searching for openings in contention with cedars, pines, sassafras, sumacs, and oaks.

In snow, the cedars and other evergreens seem compact and condensed, a tight accumulation of limbs and leaves that can perform photosynthesis year-round. The cherries, though, have a brief seasonal window of sun, and they make the most of it. Their limbs reach around and through the thicket, making the trees seem ungainly and off-balance, like a seven-foot basketball player caught by the camera in an awkward move.

I climbed over fallen trees, tripped occasionally over concealed tangles of honeysuckle, and reached a dry hedgerow ditch, where I sat down, wishing I had brought another orange. I thought of clam chowder and cornbread. Around me, white-throated sparrows and yellow-rumped warblers were working hard; perhaps their enthusiasm, like mine, was intensified by the snowfall.

I walked down the ditch until it became covered with fallen trees, then climbed out and continued on to the house site. I looked at the standing chimney and fireplace of the old kitchen. Initials had long ago been carved into various bricks. The firebox was dry and clean, and I felt certain that somewhere up the flue, on a shelf of rotting brick, a raccoon was sleeping.

I completed my itinerary with a visit to the cemetery, which has become part of my ritual on visits to Bellevue Farm. In the Parramores' time here on the farm, they would have been hitching up a pony and sleigh right now. The children would be looking forward to snow cream for dessert. The men might go down to the creek with shotguns and

Peter Ring © 1996

hope to find a few black ducks sheltered in the lee of the woods.

As for myself, I brushed the snow from the windshield of the truck, kicked what I could from my boots, and started home. As I drove down the field road, the tires made a dry, crunching sound as they left marks in the snow. In the mirror, the tracks disappeared as I drove away; ahead of me, the snow was still clean, fresh, and unbroken.

Sick Call

I've been sick for a while but am doing better now. Last Tuesday I jogged two miles at an easy pace and felt as good as any middle-aged man has a right to expect.

And then on Wednesday I awoke with a headache and chills, an elevated temperature, body aches, and general listlessness. It took an effort to walk across the room. I made a trip to the store for ginger ale and Tylenol, which I lived on for most of last week.

But, as I said, I'm better now, and ready to get back to Bellevue Farm. It is early March, and this morning a warm front brought a heavy bank of fog. Schools opened two hours late, so Tom and I decided to go down to the farm for a walk before meeting the school bus.

I like the look of fog, and so took the camera with me. Fog is a great aid to photographers because it eliminates background clutter. It softens shadows, prevents highlights from burning out, and generally diffuses the quality of light. The entire gray sky becomes a light source, not just a single spotlight sun.

I photographed the old cemetery, the house site, and some interesting trees that lay twisted in the thickets. In the fog, isolated from their background, limbs looked like body parts, arthritic and painful, dappled and flecked with lichens and moss, knotted where unsuccessful branches had made a fitful start.

Tom was walking too fast and I felt depleted. A thin glaze of perspiration formed on my forehead. I paused, waiting for my energy to return, and contemplated the empty gray sky. In the distance a Canada goose honked, and then another, until there was a chorus. They'd just arisen from a field of winter wheat. Nearby, a woodpecker drummed on a deadfall, likely advertising for a mate.

Last week I lay in bed without moving, on my back, legs straight, arms crossed across my chest. It was the only comfortable position I could find. Once I was in bed, the chills would stop, and I tried once, as an experiment, to summon up a sexual thought; indeed, I went through my Rolodex of erotic thoughts, but to no avail. I made it probably to the Cs or Ds and then was asleep, in a flu-induced slumber for some four hours, dreaming crazy things. Tom and I were on Tangier Island, which lies in the middle of the Chesapeake Bay. We were with a group of lawyers who were leaving the island by plane, but we decided to stay for a while. I told them I would fly a private plane back later. But I realized, as the gloom of evening began to fall, I did not know how to fly a plane.

And then I was back in college, Emory & Henry, in southwest Virginia, which I had attended for four years without receiving a degree because I spent more time partying

than studying. I was back, not as a callow nineteen-year-old, but as a fortysomething old fart, determined to right wrongs.

I think people from remote, rural areas such as Virginia's Eastern Shore, where I grew up, carry with them a certain expectation of failure. Academically, there were questions of whether we could compete with students from richer, better equipped city schools. We had very little lab equipment for science courses; there were no art classes, no music, no vocational courses. And we saw ourselves as backward socially as well as academically, lacking the sophistication of kids raised in urban settings such as Lynchburg, Roanoke, and Richmond.

I compensated by partying, by dating when others were studying, by drinking strange alcoholic concoctions made from recipes in *Playboy* magazine. I exhibited a certain nonchalance toward academic work, a pattern of failure to hide my fear of failure.

After four years at Emory & Henry I enlisted in the Air Force, and with the Vietnam War still raging, I figured I was one step ahead of the draft board. In the Air Force I became a photographer and traveled a great deal, and I learned in a few months what college did not teach me, that where you come from does not matter. Indeed, there were others, who did not know me well, who might have mistaken me for being somewhat worldly.

So after the Air Force I went back to college with some resolve and, working part-time at a newspaper to support myself, made the dean's list, got my degree, and fully enjoyed the process of learning. But I still have this dream of returning to Emory & Henry, and it occurs not just during a fever coma.

Weakness, I tell myself, is all in the mind. I forced myself to stand and followed Tom down the path toward Channel

Point. My legs were fine, but there was a more general weakness, and a worry that this might not soon go away.

It did, reluctantly, leaving me with a raspy cough, but my energy slowly returned and I began again the ritual of walking the field road of Bellevue Farm, the path to Channel Point, the marsh edge, the house site.

An illness, even a brief and nonserious one, reminds me that life is not without end. Like the death of a friend, it is a reminder that we all have our margins, both near and far. If there is something you want to do, now is the time to do it. I could think of a lot of exciting things to do, but for now I'm happy walking the fields and woods of Bellevue Farm, making small discoveries, such as the way a dead cedar looks when isolated by fog. There could be more to life, but there could be much less.

Pishing and Persimmons

In my four years of exploring Bellevue Farm, I have learned a few things. To wit:

Making pishing sounds to attract birds is wrong.

I rarely do it when I'm alone anymore. I prefer to sit quietly and watch birds go about their lives uninterrupted, without the panic of a human-induced air raid siren. I must admit, though, that if I am at Chincoteague National Wildlife Refuge on a Sunday, and there are a bunch of tourists around, I'll pish up a flock of yellow-rumped warblers. It is a form of showing off, of demonstrating to your companions what a great naturalist you are. Nature man! He talks with the animals! He knows the language of birds!

I doubt whether pishing endangers the birds, except perhaps when they are nesting, but it makes the observation of wild animals unnatural and dishonest. I found this out not long ago when I was sitting on a ditchbank in a hedgerow, watching palm warblers, yellow-rumps, and Carolina wrens bathe in a shallow pool of water. The birds were busy going about their daily lives, and I was happy watching them. They would bathe, drink, and then head back to the farm field, where they were feeding.

And then, for some reason, I pished. The warblers ended their bath and instantly flew to the bare limbs of an oak tree, ready for battle. Within seconds they were joined by about a dozen of their cousins, and secondary troops were coming in, stationing themselves in a persimmon tree. A chickadee fussed at me. It took about fifteen minutes for things to return to normal.

Sometimes, I think, you can communicate with birds without panicking them. Last week I heard a hermit thrush in a myrtle thicket, but I could not get a glimpse of the bird. I imitated, as best I could, the clucking sound the thrush was making, sucking air through my back teeth. After a few clucks, the thrush appeared, looking around inquisitively, expecting either a rival or a potential mate. The bird perched on a sunlit branch for a few precious seconds, and I enjoyed my look at him.

When you sit on a ditchbank in a hedgerow, don't sit in one place for too long.

Even in the dead of winter, ticks and chiggers can be active. Put your big warm butt on a community of hibernating chiggers, and pretty soon they think it's spring. Then they go looking for a blood meal.

The best way to get good persimmons is to kick the tree.

Ripe persimmons are ready to fall, and all they need is a little encouragement. When you kick the tree, the ones that

are ripest will fall readily, and if you're a good persimmon kicker you can catch them before they hit the ground.

Don't climb the tree and pick persimmons, and resist the temptation to pluck them off low branches. You'll get unripe ones that will turn your mouth to chalk dust. Possums eat a lot of persimmons, and you know what possums look like. Eat an unripe persimmon and you'll know why possums look the way they do, and why they hang from their tails.

I have been told since I was a child that it is okay to eat persimmons after the first frost of winter, but my experience proves otherwise. Persimmons have to be ripe, regardless of frost. Kick the tree, catch the persimmon, pull back the stem end, and open the skin. Press the sweet, cool orange flesh gently into your mouth.

I have learned how not to hunt.

When I first began going to Bellevue Farm, I hunted quail. But there were precious few quail on the farm, and I

Peter Ring © 1996

figured that the few remaining birds had more right to be there than I did. So I stopped carrying a shotgun, and two years ago I gave my bird dog to a friend who still hunts.

The bird dog's name is Smoke, and he is crazy. We called him Smokey Dopey, and then, for some reason, changed it to Smoke Head. For equally unknown reasons we extended the name to the rest of the family. Tom became Tom Head, his mother Mommy Head, and I'm Daddy Head.

Smoke, though crazy, is a good bird dog. Let him out of the truck and he's gone, searching for the intoxicating scent of quail with the urgency of an addict in need of a fix. He is a friendly dog, but not a social animal like the old black Lab we had before him. Smoke is very smart when it comes to learning how and where to find quail, but he would not be housebroken for the same single-minded reason he is a good bird dog. The issue of whether to shit on the floor had nothing at all to do with finding quail, so to Smoke it wasn't worth learning.

Honeysuckle climbs clockwise.

When I stopped carrying the shotgun, I needed a replacement, and I began making walking sticks from sassafras and sumac saplings. My favorites are the ones I find along the edges of hedgerows, where sufficient sunlight encourages honeysuckle growth.

If I can find a sapling with about four year's growth of honeysuckle around it, I have the makings of a wonderful walking stick. Honeysuckle grows up the sapling in a clockwise direction, and as the tree grows in circumference and the honeysuckle continues upward, the sapling develops a spiral shape, with the vine cutting into the flesh of the wood.

I cut promising saplings, allow them to season, and then

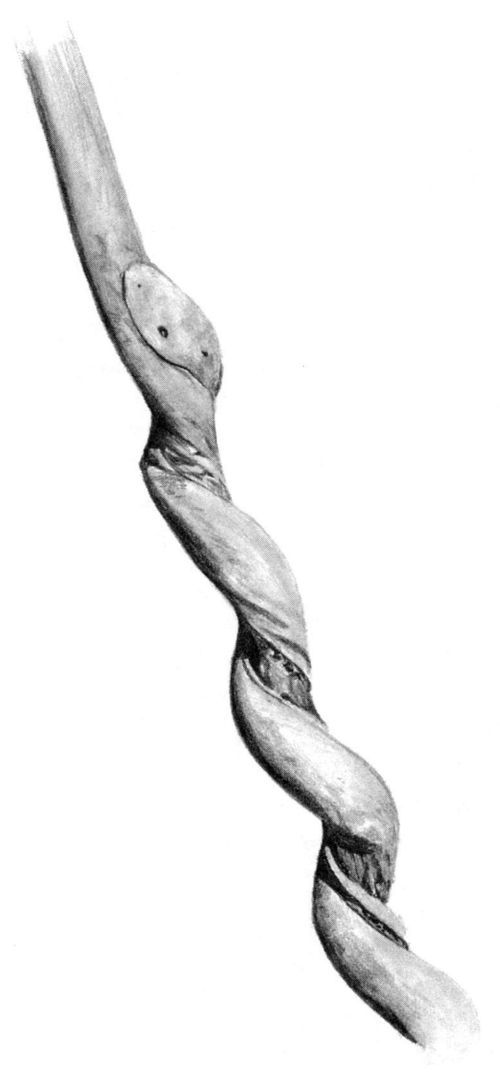

Peter Ring ©1996

take the bark off with my pocketknife and a rasp. A light sanding and an application of linseed oil finish the stick. If I intend the stick to be a functional walking stick, I glue the brass end of a spent shotgun shell onto the bottom to prevent splintering.

I've learned, from observing and cutting dozens of sticks, that honeysuckle always grows in a clockwise direction. I've asked several plant experts about this and got a variety of answers. One told me that this is because of the earth's rotation; in the Southern Hemisphere the honeysuckle would grow counterclockwise. Another told me that honeysuckle grows clockwise because the plant follows the direction of sunlight.

But I've observed other vines—fox grape, poison ivy, Virginia creeper—and they seem to climb, or not to climb, in an arbitrary manner. Sometimes they go straight up, sometimes clockwise, sometimes counterclockwise.

Robert Stiffler, garden columnist with the *Norfolk Virginian-Pilot* newspaper, explained that honeysuckle's habit of growing clockwise is a matter of genetics. It is programmed to do so, just as some people are programmed to be right-handed and some left-handed.

Whatever. It does produce a great walking stick.

Foxes eat wasps.

Some days ago I found a fox's den dug into the side of an earthen dike, and so I decided to spend some time watching for the fox. I staked out the den for several days, but the fox did not appear.

Then, just before dusk one day, as I was walking the marsh edge and heading for home, I saw her. She was some fifty feet from her den and was pawing at something on the dike. I thought at first that she had caught a rice rat or a field mouse, but I could see no other animal through the binoculars. She would paw the ground, as if digging, and then appear to feed. I watched until dark, with no clue as to what the fox was doing.

Recently I walked out to the dike and searched the area where the fox had been feeding, expecting to find the remains of some small animal, but I found nothing. Then, following her tracks through the sand, I found what she had been pawing at. It was a nest of paper wasps that, according to the dimensions of the hole, was about the size of a basketball.

The fox must have picked up the scent of the nest as she was traveling near her den and decided to have a dinner of wasp larvae. She had carefully dug it out, and bits and pieces of paper nest were scattered downhill. A small part of the nest, with larvae still in their compartments, remained in the hole. The fox, apparently, was saving them for another day.

Black feathers are stronger than white feathers.

In summer, when the presence of mosquitoes, ticks, and chiggers makes walking in the woods of Bellevue impossible, I walk along the marshy shoreline and small beaches of Burton's Bay. Here I find all kinds of things. Shells, bones, egg casings of whelks and skates, grasses, garbage, and bird feathers.

In finding feathers on the beach, I have noticed that black feathers are stronger than white ones. When I find a black-tipped feather from a snow goose or ring-billed gull, the white areas will often be worn away while the black tip remains intact. This is why birds that live around the water usually have black wing tips. When a gull, for example, takes off from Burton's Bay, its wings beat the water on the first

Peter Ring ©1996

few strokes. Were it not for those strong black wing tips, the flight feathers would soon be broken and the bird's ability to fly diminished.

Nearly all gulls and terns have black tips or trailing edges on their wings. Many seabirds are dark all over. The cormorant, a poor flier that beats its wings unmercifully on take-off, is a good example.

The gannet is a beautiful white seabird that dives for its dinner. It has black wing tips. Ditto the osprey. Black vultures and turkey vultures, which make their living on land, are dark, but the trailing edges of their wings are lighter.

Fall: The Reawakening

They tell us that fall is a dark time, a time of decay and foreboding, when cold rains strip the trees bare, turn the earth sodden, chill us to the bone. Fall, the precursor of winter, an unfriendly season that must be endured before we are allowed the rebirth of spring.

But at Bellevue Farm, fall is a time of reawakening. The oaks, sweet gums, and wild cherry trees that line the hedgerows and forests drop their leaves, making the woods once again accessible. The clouds of mosquitoes that swarmed over the low areas have gone, and the ticks and chiggers have become dormant. In summer I explored the farm by canoe, plying each of the little creeks and guts as far as I could, pushing the boat into the salt marsh until its gunwales were locked by cordgrass, and thousands of little midges would leave the grass and alight on my bare, sweaty legs. Now I can again walk the hedgerows, sit in the dry ditches, search for fatwood stumps, and track the old fox whose den is on the earthen dike where dredge spoil was dumped years ago.

Fall for me is not a precursor to winter's death on Bellevue; it is not a time of suppression and darkness. It is a time of life, as if the curtain is rising on a new season. Fall is the initiation, the nativity.

I watch a northern harrier glide over the soybean field, hunting field mice, and I experience the feeling of reunion. When did I last see the harrier? March? April?

A red-tailed hawk soars overhead and turkey vultures circle on thermals, sniffing out deer parts poachers have left behind. Yes, we have poachers. They cruise these back roads at night with spotlights, temporarily blind deer as they feed on winter wheat, shoot them, and then quickly retrieve the quivering carcasses, slide them into the beds of their pickup trucks, cover them with tarps, and take them home to butcher in some bloody toolshed where the curtains are drawn.

The quick response to these people is revulsion, but for some, venison is winter meat and the killing of a deer is not sport, but survival. Some sell their venison in black markets in the cities. This I can understand. Venison is plentiful. Cash is in short supply here in the country, especially in winter when work on the water is hard to come by. Selling venison is a shady form of capitalism, illegal but better than food stamps. Here in the country we value our independence, and welfare still carries a stigma, meaning that as individuals we have failed. Thirty days in the county jail on poaching charges is preferable, meaning not that we have failed, but have fallen victim to bad luck.

The poachers I can't abide are those who kill for the sake of killing. A six-pack and a thirty-thirty. A perfectly good deer left to rot in the fields. I have found those deer steaming in the morning sunlight, rotting away until the vultures are called by a scent on the wind, a death notice rising on a thermal.

I like best the gray days of late fall, early December northeasters that turn the bay the color of lead, rain that pelts dead leaves, cold winds that send the juncos scurrying into the underbrush, foraging for food with obvious urgency. It is a time of excitement, intimations of winter, the heart races, there are things to do, preparations to be made.

On late afternoons I walk the marsh, wearing my old waxed cotton jacket with the familiar smell of a canvas tent. The salt-meadow hay has turned brown, and the seedpods of sea oxeye are dark and prickly, somehow even more beautiful in their winter mode than when they bloomed yellow in August, but in winter these seedheads are distinctive, and here in the marsh they seem especially fitting—hardy and robust, spartan and functional, holding in abeyance potential life.

A northeast wind raises froth on Burton's Bay. Little breakers smack the shoreline, tearing at the peat banks that once were high marsh. Ribbed mussels grow in clusters. Sometimes they are torn free by storm tides, and later, at low tide, their shells can be found littered along the berm seaward of the peat bogs.

I like a good wind. It is energizing, even in the discomfort it brings. My cheeks grow numb, as do my ears. I pull up the hood of my sweatshirt, tighten the drawstring, flip up the collar of my jacket, stuff my hands into the felt-lined pockets and feel there a few .22 shells left over from target shooting last winter. I juggle them in my fingers and feel the thin waxy coating on the blunt lead bullets. I feel warmer, my face stings,

Peter Ruiz © 1996

my legs feel strong. I enjoy the squish of the firm wet mud, something sexual about it, the sound, the cadence of my footsteps, an ongoing rhythm like a pulse, breaking into the steady rush of the wind, the lick of the surf, the barking of brant far out on the mudflats of Burton's Bay.

It is the brant that mark the season and make it certain. They nested in the far Arctic over the summer, and now they are back, their white rumps bobbing in the chop of the bay. They sound like puppies, a high-pitched bark that is kind to the ear, a wonderful sound that defines winter here on the seaside. I see them flying in ragged strings low to the water, barking gently in that sweet brant voice that sounds like no other waterfowl. And suddenly I'm reminded—that is what I like so much about being out here.

I take a pee, steam rising from my urine stream, from the little puddle I leave at the woods edge. My hands are cold. I decide to walk back to the truck through the woods where it will be warm in islands of sunlight, away from the wind. But first I sit on the trunk of a red cedar that fell during a summer storm, and I reach into the game pocket of my jacket for an orange, the first of the season. I cut it into quarters with my pocketknife, wipe the blade on my pants, and stretch out my legs.

The orange is sweet and juicy, and I make a note to buy more from the same store. Some oranges can be pulpy and have little juice, a disappointment after you've hiked the marsh for two hours and are looking forward to sitting on a cedar log and having a reward. This one is good. I first lick the juices off the quarters, then bite into the flesh and use my front teeth to peel the pulp from the skin. I spit the seeds at a brown mushroom growing at the base of a pin oak.

In the woods, out of the wind, the birds are busy. Nervous little yellow-rumped warblers flitter through the wax myrtle thickets, eating gray berries. Their little yellow butts stand out clearly, even on a cloudy day. Butter butts, I call them. There are northern cardinals, juncos, wrens, downy woodpeckers, northern flickers, and towhees, all within a short distance of where I am sitting. I either see them or hear them.

The wooded path, unused through the summer, has grown up some, but the grasses are dying back, the leaves falling and becoming matted on the ground, and the woods is opening up again. In summer it is dense and claustrophobic, sweltering and thick with insects. Now it is becoming open and light, and I can see the salt marsh and Finney Creek on the other side of the forest.

In the nearness of winter, I sense the reawakening of the forest and salt marsh, the busy commerce of the birds, the conversations of the brant, the hunts of the red-tailed hawk, and I feel excitement at once again being here, as once again life has broken free.

Becoming Owl-like

In the years I have been hiking Bellevue Farm, I have developed a proprietorial sense toward the place. I do not own the land, could not even afford to pay the county taxes on it, and have no legal claim whatsoever. I am here at the pleasure of The Nature Conservancy.

My territorial sense, acquired after years of prowling the myrtle thickets and marshes, is akin to that of the great horned owl that roosts in a cedar on Channel Point. My claim has to do with exploring and learning about the land and nothing at all to do with the principles of English law.

The big owl owns Channel Point, of that there can be no doubt. I regularly find regurgitated pellets under the cedar tree and break them apart with a stick. There are bones of field mice, small birds, and fur that might have belonged to a rabbit. These morsels she collected from the woods of Channel Point, the nearby fields, or the tidal flats of Burton's Bay. She knows this farm so well she can dine at leisure.

Recently I found other, more disturbing evidence of

ownership. The remains of another owl—just feathers, really—were scattered throughout the woods. I at first feared that the old she-owl had met her match, but the feathers were smaller than those of a great horned owl. They were clearly owl feathers—the trailing edges of the flight feathers had soft, downy margins to silence them on hunting flights—but the feathers probably belonged to an eastern screech owl. The screech owl had likely entered the larger owl's territory, and had lost its life in doing so.

But to deepen the mystery, as I walked along the path to the point, I came across more feathers, these from a large bird, but clearly not an owl. The flight feathers were long, slightly curved, and had hard edges. The tips of the feathers were black, with white spots running through them. A gull had met its death here, the victim of the great horned owl or perhaps a fox. It was a large gull, a great black-backed or herring gull, or maybe a ring-billed gull. All three have black wing tips with white markings. Later, I found gull feathers hanging in the limbs of a cedar tree. Clearly the kill had not been made by a fox.

The great horned owl rules a broad territory, and she accepts my visits with reluctance. Now and then I surprise her when I hike out to Channel Point, and she flies off through the tops of the pine trees, out over the marsh, and doubles back behind me to await my departure.

I have grown over time to think like the owl. I accept the presence of others on the farm with reluctance. A farm worker drove his truck down the lane to Channel Point the other day, apparently had lunch there, and left a beer can on the ground. The brand was Milwaukee's Best, a cheap beer. When I left the farm, workers were plowing the fields and their pickup trucks were parked along the dirt lane. I walked

Peter Ring ©1996

by the pickups slowly, peering into the cabs and the beds, looking for evidence that might implicate a drinker of Milwaukee's Best. I found none.

The owl knows where to find field mice and rice rats. I know where to find fatwood. I know where William Parramore's garbage dump was, where he stashed his ballast stones after loading his schooner. I know where a house wren hangs out, and I know of a spooky place among the thick old cedar trees down by the marsh where the limbs close over your head, shutting out the sunlight and making the understory seem dark, as if a storm were brewing. It's quiet in there, and in the darkness there is no undergrowth, just a soft bed of grassy tumps, a good place, it has struck me on several occasions, to have sex.

I have sometimes, on warm spring days, taken off my clothes and waded in the cold water of Burton's Bay, or stretched out on the warming sand of a small beach to feel the first heat of summer. After a winter of snows and northeasters, the first heat is welcome, especially on bare skin. Lying in the sun on a warm spring day has yin-yang quality. At once I have the heat of the sun, sufficient to draw beads of sweat to my brow, and with it a cool lick of breeze fresh off the cold bay. Hot and cold. Summer and winter. The sun brings intimations of summer, and the breeze harbors the remnants of winter. The sand I lie on is warm, and its grit feels good against my skin. But when I wade in the water, I find that the bay is still numbingly cold.

I find these contrasts very appealing, and I enjoy the process of shedding clothes. It is a ritual I have developed, a way of welcoming summer, to feel for the first time in months the heat of the sun on my skin. It is the best way to experience the change of the seasons, and like watching birds and searching for stone tools, it brings me closer to Bellevue Farm and reinforces my proprietorship, making me feel, like the owl, that I belong here.

It also is a process of liberation to lie here on the sand without clothes. I am, after all, from a family of conservative Protestant people, who rarely over the generations, I suppose, have enjoyed the magic of feeling owl-like, especially if it meant taking off one's clothes where there was a chance, even if slim, that they might be seen by a stranger.

I am from a family of southerners who, following the Civil War, became good people. They were not bad people before the war, as far as I know, but after the war they had little land, less money, and what hope they had came through the scriptures. And so, like many southern families, they became good people. And when I was growing up, in the 1950s, my parents and grandparents often reminded me that we were, although not well off, good people.

I once asked my grandmother what the term meant, and she only laughed, as if it were beyond a child's grasp to understand such things, and so I came upon my own definition, based upon implication rather than fact. Considering oneself good people seems at first glance to portend a certain arrogance, but in the southern way of my grandmother, being good people did not mean that one valued oneself above others—good people would never be so presumptuous—but that you lived your life according to certain values and standards, certain manners.

Good people embraced the church and the teachings of Christ. We went to Sunday school and stayed for preaching. We wore starched shirts and neckties and carried Bibles with Jesus' words printed in red. Our Bibles were the King James version and had pages in the front where we listed the family genealogy. The symbolic closeness of God and family was not lost on us.

Good people always said grace before meals and prayed before retiring for the night, yet we refrained from being overtly religious. Religion was to be practiced in moderation and with restraint. Church attendance was mandatory, but it was considered bad manners to be demonstrative. Those who danced about and shouted with joy when Jesus came into their hearts were . . . well, they weren't good people.

Good people loved the classic hymns—"Trust and Obey," "What a Friend We Have in Jesus," "The Old Rugged Cross"—and sang them accompanied by piano or organ, never guitar or brass instruments. The women hummed them softly as they prepared the chicken and potatoes for Sunday dinner.

In good families, a man always stood when a woman entered a room. He offered his chair, was deferential and reverent to his elders. A man said "sir" to older men, and to men of his own age or younger for whom he had respect. A boy learned early to shake hands with a firm grip and to look you in the eye.

Good people knew the value of work and education. If a job was to be done, it was to be done right. Good people were honest and thrifty. They did business with a handshake and paid their bills on time. They joined the Ruritans and the Missionary Society and held great pride in their community.

Good people were stoic in the face of illness and loss. Although family members were allowed their contentions, at a time of tragedy the family always came together to offer succor and sustenance. A terminal illness was a family matter, not one for a hospital.

Good people performed the same service for friends in time of trouble, whether it was something as simple as showing up with a plate of deviled eggs or reading to an ill neighbor.

Surprisingly, I found that my grandmother's definition of good people was supremely democratic. It could be applied to rich or poor, black or white. The definition knew no cultural boundaries; the only standard seemed to be longevity. If the family had lived according to certain standards and manners for a certain number of generations, then they were good people.

Conversely, I can't remember my grandmother ever describing anyone as bad people, although it was apparent she did not approve of the actions of some. Her favorite expression, one that summed up her definition of social hierarchy, was "Water seeks its level." She said it with finality, implying that social actions are the manifestations of natural law.

My grandmother would not approve of my lying here on the sand without clothes, but I find in doing it a certain emancipation, a middle-age renegotiation of my Baptist upbringing. Sexuality was not discussed in our house when I was growing up; my father and I had no father and son talks. So what information and misinformation I came by was gleaned from older kids who were but slightly less in the dark than I was. We were a community of Protestants, of good people.

So owl-like I lie here on an unknown beach on Bellevue Farm, coarse sand embedding itself in my backside. I am learning, at long last, what I am. And what I am is a territorial animal, a creature who knows these woods better than anyone, and who thus owns them. No one else knows of this place. It is mine. Mine and the owl's.

APPENDIX A

The Parramores

The first Parramores came to America as indentured servants, but by the time of the Revolution they were among the leaders of the growing Virginia colony. John Parramore arrived in 1622 aboard the *Bona Venture* as a seventeen-year-old servant to John Blower. By the 1630s, Parramore's name was appearing regularly in court documents, ranging in nature from litigation over business transactions to a charge of cursing on the Sabbath. By the early 1640s Parramore was thriving to the point where he had an indentured servant of his own, Edward Robins.

By 1650, Parramore was living on a 200-acre plantation in Northampton County on Magothy Bay, some thirty miles south of Bellevue Farm. He later bought a 250-acre farm on Occohannock Creek on the Chesapeake Bay. On November 9, 1666, Parramore patented 1,500 acres in northern Accomack County near the Maryland line, and then had to repeat the patent process with Maryland in 1668 when Virginia gave up its claim to the area. Parramore thus named the plantation "Double Purchase." He died there in 1676.

Thomas Parramore, a grandson of John, married the widow Joanna Custis Hope, granddaughter of William Custis, younger brother of Major General John Custis. Joanna inherited the Bellevue land, including what would become Parramore Island, from her grandfather, who had purchased it from the original patent holder, Edmund Scarburgh.

Thomas survived Joanna and when he died in 1774 left Bellevue to his son William, "my heir apparent." A second son, John, was given land in Maryland, and Thomas, the third son, was bequeathed land in Northampton County.

This from Thomas's will: "I give and bequeath unto my son William Parramore my Negro Robin Shoe Maker but to be obliged to make twenty pair of shoes for each of the families of Major Guy, Ezekiel Young, John Parramore, and William Holland every year as long as he is able to work and also for my son Thomas Parramore's family the same quantity each year, when my said son Thomas gets a family."

William was a prominent man in the community and in 1777 was one of the justices who transferred allegiance from the Crown to the Commonwealth of Virginia. He was a colonel of the militia in the Revolution and, in the years following the war, became a deeply religious man who grew to detest slavery. In 1787 he issued a deed of manumission freeing his ten slaves: "I, William Parramore, being fully convinced of the just and equal right that all human nature have to the happy enjoyment of personal liberty, as well as that the slavery of our fellow creatures is repugnant to and a violation of our blessed Christian religion, have and hereby do manumitt, set free, and discharge my several negro slaves, to wit, Jacob Bemane, Issac Wan, Phillis Roan, Phillis Anthony,

Stephen Moses, Caleb Brister, Abel Daniel, Tabitha Christopher, Ezebella Joshua, Esther Roan; and for as much of the introduction of the above mentioned negroes into society make a second name necessary for their distinction from other negroes who have been or may be hereafter liberated, I have added the names above as a second name to each of them respectively."

The first wife of William was Sarah, the daughter of Digby and Rose Seymour, and she was the mother of his two sons, William, Jr., and Thomas. She died in 1802, and by the next year he had married another Sarah, who survived him. William and the first Sarah are buried in the family cemetery at Bellevue Farm.

The Parramore family served its community and country with distinction. Thomas Parramore was first elected to the House of Burgesses in 1748 and reelected thirteen times before his death in the 1770s. His oldest son, William, was an Accomack County justice and a trustee of Garrison's Chapel when it was built in 1787. William's son, Thomas, was a colonel in the Revolutionary army.

This letter was written in 1781 to Virginia governor Nelson from Colonel John Cropper, leader of the local militia: "A volunteer troop of horses have been assembled under the command of Col. Thomas Parramore; this corps is chiefly composed of single young gentlemen and they are gentlemen of the first fortunes and characters among us." Thomas was seventeen at the time.

Four Parramores served in the Virginia legislature, beginning with Thomas's tenure of some twenty-five years in the House of Burgesses and running through the Civil War. Thomas Custis Parramore was a member of the House during that war, and he became judge of the county court in 1870.

William R. Parramore was a physician who practiced in Accomac in the 1880s.

The plantation home at Bellevue was built in 1818 by Thomas Parramore, son of William, who inherited the property in 1816, according to Ralph T. Whitelaw, author of *Virginia's Eastern Shore,* published in 1951. Whitelaw wrote that the plantation was referred to as Bellevue in the 1816 will, and that a more modest residence, presumably the home of William and Sarah, was on the property at the time the larger home was constructed.

Thomas and his wife, Mary Darby, built a large two-story home with fine millwork and detailing. In its day, it was no doubt a showplace. From Whitelaw: "The house today has two brick ends and in the west wall is a brick dated 1818 and set in the wall are large wrought iron initials T and P, so apparently it was erected by Thomas Parramore shortly after his inheritance. The cornice under the eaves is ornamented with modillions, alternating with five-pointed stars, below which is a row of carved scrollwork. The lintels are of wood. The eaves of the front porch and the pediment have similar modillions and scrolls, on a reduced scale, but no stars. The pilars are round and fluted. Each of the double entrance doors has five sets of graduated super-imposed panels. The rear porch has square fluted columns and scroll carving on the pediment, but no modillions.

"From the front porch the entrance is into a large square hall with the stairs in the front corner; as they pass the windows in the front and end walls, the hand rail and banisters are duplicated along the walls, perhaps as a safety precaution. The hall has a chair rail and wainscoting and a plaster decoration about the chandelier suspension hook in the ceiling.

"The formal room is behind the entrance hall and has an outside entrance from the rear porch. Besides the chair rail and wainscoting similar to that in the hall, it has a deep plaster cornice and a more ornate ceiling decoration. To the left of the hall is the dining room and behind the latter a first-floor chamber, but it has no door to the formal room next to it. Both of those rooms have wainscoting and plaster cornice . . .

"The house has been unoccupied and exposed to the elements for years, so that it is in a sad state of dilapidation, in spite of the fact that visiting architects had said that besides possessing rare beauty of interior finish it is one of the most soundly built houses that they have ever observed."

Parramore Island

In 1686 a patent was given to William Custis for eight hundred acres on "Feaks his Island." In 1726 Custis left it to his granddaughter, Joanna, and she married Thomas Parramore. Thomas inherited the island, along with the Bellevue plantation, upon her death.

In 1687 Isaac Metcalfe patented one hundred acres called Isaac's Beach "in the inlet between Cedar and Feches and now adjoining Feches." It was sold to Thomas Parramore in 1750.

Whitelaw writes that in the 1700s maps began to identify the island as Teach's Island, perhaps on the assumption that it had been a haunt of Edward Teach, otherwise known as Blackbeard the Pirate. "However, the 1673 map of Augustine Herrman called it Fetche's Island, and as this was long before the days of Blackbeard, it seems reasonable that Teach's was a phonetic corruption of Fetche's."

After Thomas left the island to his son William, a 1787 survey showed 1,150 acres exclusive of the adjacent marsh.

Through purchases, and by accretion, Parramore Island had become one of the largest barrier beaches on the mid-Atlantic held by one owner.

In 1816 William left the island to his sons Thomas and William, and various Parramore heirs owned it until 1871, when Parramore Island and the adjacent salt marsh were sold to Tallmadge F. Cherry of Baltimore. Other individual owners followed, and in 1892 Duncan C. Anderson of Big Stone Gap sold to the Parramore Land and Improvement Company, which operated a hunting club on the island.

According to Whitelaw, in 1917 the corporation sold to Edward P. Timmons of Philadelphia, and three years later he and his wife sold to the Fox Island Association, Inc. In 1921 the name of the holding company was changed to Parramore Island Association and three years later to the Parramore Island Development Company, and the club was called Holly Island Club.

A clubhouse was situated on the north end of the island but was severely damaged in the storm of 1933. Because of the chaotic economic times, it was never fully rebuilt. Part of the clubhouse was moved to the middle of the island on the inner side.

In 1935 the property was sold by a trustee, some private transactions followed, and it was then purchased by Dr. Carl Schmidlapp of New York, who sold the island to The Nature Conservancy in 1973.

Dr. Schmidlapp, an ardent conservationist, was dedicated to preserving the island in its natural state, which before the sale to the Conservancy appeared increasingly unlikely. In 1955 the U.S. Navy announced plans to take Parramore by condemnation and convert it to a bombing range. Public opposition stopped that project, but in the 1960s rumors were circulating that the state would condemn the island and build a park there.

The Nature Conservancy and Dr. Schmidlapp and his associates, after years of negotiating, struck a deal. The Conservancy would pay $1.6 million for the island and adjacent marsh, and the former owners would retain use rights for twenty years.

The Schmidlapp family for years had a hunting club in an abandoned U.S. Lifesaving Service station, but the building was struck by lightning in the late 1980s and burned to the ground. The U.S. Coast Guard maintained a station on Parramore until the fall of 1994, when it moved its operation to the mainland. Today Parramore has no permanent human residents and is only visited by a few graduate students conducting island research or local school groups on field trips.

APPENDIX B

Accomacs, Occohannocks, and Others

Little is known about the Indians that inhabited the Eastern Shore of Virginia prior to contact with Europeans. There have been no major archaeological sites and we have no written records before the visit by Captain John Smith in 1608.

Smith wrote that there were two major tribes on the Eastern Shore: the Accomacs and the Occohannocks, both of which had loose ties with the Powhatan nation, which in the late 1500s and early 1600s ruled much of what is now southeastern Virginia. Subsequent visits showed that the Indians of the Eastern Shore were not just one or two closely organized groups, but rather a large number of small communities, a fact that is reflected in the large number of communities on the Eastern Shore today that have Indian names.

Most experts on Eastern Shore Indians believe the earliest residents were nomadic hunter-gatherers who lived off the abundant natural resources of the creeks and shallow bays of the seaside and bayside. With waters teeming with fish and shellfish, there was little need to clear land, plant crops, and form tightly governed communities. We do know that by the early 1600s, though, Eastern Shore Indians were planting and harvesting corn, both for their own use and for trade with tribes across the bay. Thomas Savage, one of the earliest European landowners on the Eastern Shore, reported that "forty great canowes" were used to ship corn to the Powhatans.

John Smith probably had little contact, if any, with the Indians that lived along the seaside creeks and bays. The population was spread out and there were no major cities, as described in an article in the *Peninsula Enterprise* in 1900 by Thomas Teakle Upshur. Smith did an admirable job as an anthropologist, but his chief mission was the defense of the Jamestown colony, which he commanded. So Smith's primary interest in local Indians dealt with the degree to which they could pose a threat to Jamestown. He found little to fear on the Eastern Shore.

The local Indians traded regularly with the Powhatans, and probably with the tribes that preceded them. The favored items of trade were the shells of clams and mussels, and especially the disk-shaped beads made from these shells, called *roanoke* or *peak*. Such beads can still sometimes be found in local farm fields. In return, local Indians likely received stone and metal tools, weapons, and perhaps grain. By the 1600s, Eastern Shore Indians were growing enough corn to export, and this industry probably was introduced to local tribes through trade contacts with western ones.

Indians of the Eastern Shore are described in most reports as friendly and welcoming toward whites, a fact that likely was grounded as much in economics as in a benevolent nature. In the 1620s the English began supplanting the Powhatans as trading partners for Eastern Shore Indians, and the decision by local tribes not to participate in a war against the English in

1622 likely was made in what would have passed in those years for the corporate boardroom.

The English had no desire to seize Indian land on the Eastern Shore, but rather to develop a strong trading network centered around furs, grain, salt, fish, and other commodities. Settlement did come, however, and by the late 1600s few of the small villages remained. The Gingaskin reservation in Northampton, which had at one time been one of the largest, was reduced to 650 acres. Encroachment by whites took its toll, but even more damaging was disease, especially smallpox, introduced by foreign sailors.

Robert Beverley wrote in 1705 that the scattered villages of Eastern Shore Indians had become mere remnants. The Matchopungoes were once one of the largest tribes, with several villages on the seaside between Wachapreague and Brownsville, but in 1705 only a few families remained. The few remaining Gingoteagues, Beverley wrote, had joined a Maryland tribe. The Occohannocks had few living members, and the remaining Chiconessex only "kept the name alive."